WEATHER FOR KIDS

WIND, RAIN, THUNDER & LIGHTNING
CHILDREN'S SCIENCE & NATURE

BABY PROFESSOR

EDUCATION KIDS

Speedy Publishing LLC

40 E. Main St. #1156

Newark, DE 19711

www.speedypublishing.com

Copyright 2016

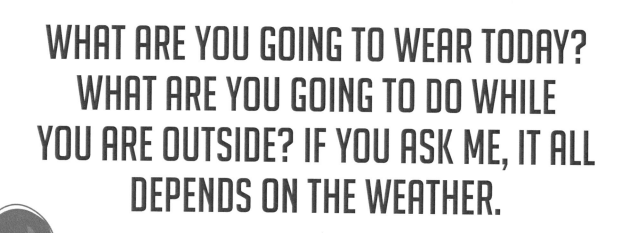

WHAT ARE YOU GOING TO WEAR TODAY?
WHAT ARE YOU GOING TO DO WHILE
YOU ARE OUTSIDE? IF YOU ASK ME, IT ALL
DEPENDS ON THE WEATHER.

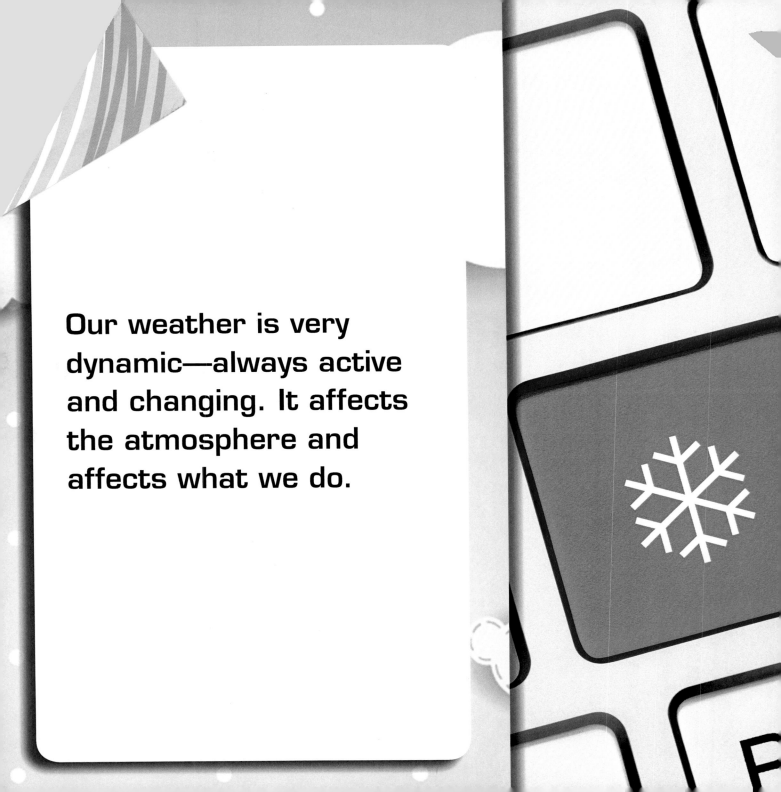

Our weather is very dynamic—always active and changing. It affects the atmosphere and affects what we do.

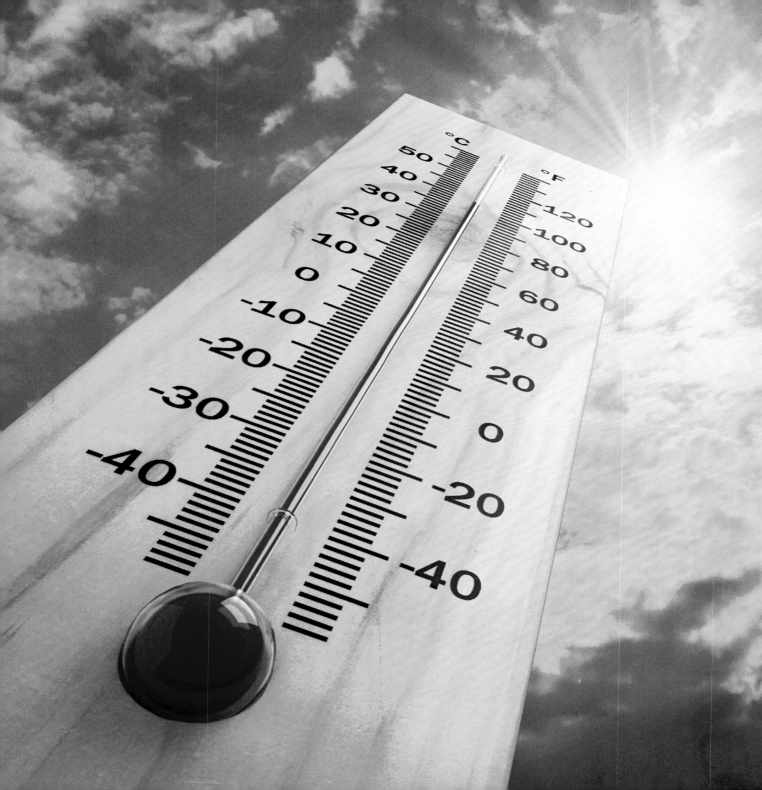

Do you ever wonder what and how some weather elements are created that affect our daily condition outside?

Thunder and Lightning. We will hear a kaboom! Exciting for me, scary for some. Both go together. They're inseparable.

Lightning makes the thunder. When ice and water particles hit against each other, that's when they create an electric charge above the clouds.

By the time these electrical charges connects with electrical charges from the ground, kaboom! Lightning strikes!

This is quite dangerous. News all over the world reports when lightning hits tall trees, houses, buildings, even people. Thunder happens all-year round but mostly in the afternoon or evening.

Compared to tornadoes or hurricanes, lightning strikes kill more people every year, averaging about 75 to 100 people a year.

Some say that if you hear thunder roar, it is likely that lightning will strike nearby. But in truth, you actually see a lightning strike first before hearing the sound of its thunder.

Light travels faster than sound waves. You can even see a lightning strike up to 100 miles away, while only hearing thunder sounds up to 15 miles away.

Wind and Rain. These two exist in a close relationship. Increasing rainfall may likely affect the wind.

Wind is the movement of air on Earth. Air pressure causes this. Its speed and strength also depends on air pressure.

The strength of winds comes in knots (unit of measure for winds). We rate the wind in a scale of strength: breeze, strong wind, gale, storm, and hurricane.

There are many recreational activities that use the wind, including kite boarding, sailing, wind surfing, and paragliding. And of course we can always fly a kite!

Rain, on the other hand, is part of a cycle. These are droplets of water vapor in the air.

As warm air rises in the atmosphere, it brings along with it the water droplets. As the clouds become heavier, gravity sets to work and will cause those water droplets to fall back to the ground as rain. And the cycle continues.

There are moments when all the weather elements happen simultaneously. You will feel strong winds, experience a heavy downpour of rain, hear thunder and see lightning all at the same time.

It is best to be safe when you are going to be outside. There are many types of protective gear and suitable clothes to wear when the weather's notgoing to be good for what you planned to do that day.

WEATHER

ENTER
(click here more information)

So, before you plan any trip or activity, check the weather forecast. You will go out better prepared and be able to have fun. Or, you may choose to just stay cozy indoors.

Visit

BABY PROFESSOR
EDUCATION KIDS

www.BabyProfessorBooks.com

to download Free Baby Professor eBooks
and view our catalog of new and exciting
Children's Books

Made in the USA
San Bernardino, CA
16 February 2018